KU-161-283

Seeing a Colour-Blind Future

THE PARADOX OF RACE

THE 1997 REITH LECTURES

PATRICIA J. WILLIAMS

A *Virago* book

Published by Virago Press 1997

Copyright © Patricia J. Williams 1997

The moral right of the author has been asserted

All rights reserved. No part of this publication may be
reproduced, stored in a retrieval system, or transmitted
in any form or by any means, without the prior
permission in writing of the publisher, nor be otherwise
circulated in any form of binding or cover other than
that in which it is published and without a similar
condition being imposed on the subsequent purchaser.

A CIP catalogue record for this book is available
from the British Library

ISBN 1 86049 365 3

Typeset in Plantin by M Rules
Printed and bound in Great Britain by
Clays Ltd, St Ives plc

Virago
A Division of
Little, Brown and Company (UK)
Brettenham House
Lancaster Place
London WC2E 7EN

Contents

1 The Emperor's New Clothes   *1*

2 The Pantomime of Race   *15*

3 The Distribution of Distress   *29*

4 The War Between the Worlds   *45*

5 An Ordinary Brilliance   *59*

1

The Emperor's New Clothes

My son attends a small nursery school. Over the past year, three different teachers in his school assured me that he was colour-blind. Resigned to this diagnosis, I took my son to an opthalmologist who tested him and pronounced his vision perfect. I could not figure out what was going on until I began to listen carefully to what he was saying about colour.

As it turned out, my son did not misidentify colour. He resisted identifying colour at all. 'I don't know,' he would say when asked what colour the grass was; or, most peculiarly, 'It makes no difference'. This latter remark, this assertion of the greenness of grass making no difference, was such a precociously cynical retort, that I began to suspect some social complication in which he somehow was invested.

The long and the short of it is that the well-meaning teachers at his predominantly white school had valiantly and repeatedly assured their charges that colour makes no difference. 'It doesn't matter,' they told the children, 'whether you're black or white or red or green or blue.' Yet upon further investigation, the very reason that the teachers had felt it necessary to impart this lesson in the first place was that it *did* matter, and in predictably cruel ways: some of the children had been fighting about whether black people could play 'good guys'.

My son's anxious response was redefined by his teachers as physical deficiency. This anxiety redefined as deficiency suggests to me that it may be illustrative of the way in which the liberal ideal of colour-blindness is too often confounded. That is to say, the very notion of blindness about colour constitutes an ideological confusion at best, and denial at its very worst. I recognise, certainly, that the teachers were inspired by a desire to make whole a division in the ranks. But there is much overlooked in the move to undo that which clearly and unfortunately matters just by labelling it that which 'makes no difference'. The dismissiveness, however unintentional, leaves those in my son's position pulled between the clarity of their own experience and the often alienating terms in which they must seek social acceptance.

There's a lot of that in the world right now: someone has just announced in no uncertain terms that they hate you because you're dark, let's say, or Catholic or a woman or the wrong height, and the panicked authority figures try to patch things up by reassuring you that race or gender or stature or your heartfelt religion doesn't matter; means nothing in the calculation of your humanity; is the most insignificant little puddle of beans in the world.

While I do want to underscore that I do embrace colour-blindness as a legitimate hope for the future, I worry that we tend to enshrine the notion with a kind of utopianism whose naïvety will assure its elusiveness. In the material world ranging from playgrounds to politics, our ideals perhaps need more thoughtful, albeit more complicated, guardianship. By this I mean something more than the 'I think therefore it is' school of idealism. 'I don't think about colour, therefore your problems don't exist.' If only it were so easy.

But if indeed it's not that easy then the application of such quick fixes becomes not just a shortcut but a short-circuiting of the process of resolution. In the example of my son's experience at school, the collective aversion to confronting the social tensions he faced resulted in their being pathologised as his individual physical limitation. This is a phenomenon that happens all too frequently to children of colour in a variety of contexts. In both the United States and the United Kingdom, the disproportionate numbers of black children who end up in special education or who are written off as failures attest to the degree to which this is a profound source of social anxiety.

In addition, the failure to deal straightforwardly with the pervasive practices of exclusion that infect even the very young allowed my son's white schoolmates to indulge in the false luxury of a prematurely imagined community. By this I mean that we can all be lulled rather too easily into a self-congratulatory stance of preached universalism – 'We are the world! We are the children!' was the evocative, full-throated harmony of a few years ago. Yet nowhere has that been invoked more passionately than in the face of tidal waves of dissension, and even as 'the' children learn that 'we' children are not like 'those', the benighted creatures on the other side of the pale.

This tension between material conditions and what one is cultured to see or not see – the dilemma of the emperor's new clothes, we might call it – is a tension faced by any society driven by bitter histories of imposed hierarchy. I don't mean to suggest that we need always go about feeling guilty or responsible or perpetually burdened by original sin or notions of political correctness. I do wish, however, to counsel against the facile innocence of those three notorious monkeys, Hear no evil, See no evil, and Speak no evil. Theirs is a purity achieved through ignorance. Ours must be a world in which we know each other better.

To put it another way, it is a dangerous if comprehensible temptation to imagine inclusiveness by imagining away any obstacles. It is in this way that the moral high ground of good intentions knows its limits. We must be careful not to allow our intentions to verge into outright projection by substituting a fantasy of global seamlessness that is blinding rather than just colour-blind.

This is a dilemma – being coloured, so to speak, in a world of normative whiteness – whiteness being defined as the absence of colour. The drive to conform our surroundings to whatever we know as 'normal' is a powerful force – convention in many ways is more powerful than reason, and customs in some instances are more powerful than law. While surely most customs and conventions encode the insights of ancient wisdom, the habits of racial thought in Western society just as surely encapsulate some of the greatest mistakes in human history. So how do we rethink this most troubled of divisions, the fault line in our body politic, the fault line in ourselves. The ability to remain true to *one* self seems to me to be not only an ultimate goal of our political and social aspirations but must begin with the ethical project of considering how we can align a sense of ourselves with a sense of the world. This is the essence of integrity, is it not, never having to split into a well-maintained 'front' and a closely-guarded 'inside'.

Creating community, in other words, involves this most difficult work of negotiating real divisions, of considering boundaries before we go crashing through, and of pondering our differences before we can ever agree on the terms of our sameness. For the discounted vision of the emperor's new clothes (or a little boy's colour) is already the description of corrupted community.

Perhaps one reason that conversations about race are so often doomed to frustration is that the notion of whiteness as 'race' is almost never implicated. One of the more difficult legacies of slavery and of colonialism is the degree to which racism's tenacious hold is manifested not merely in the divided demographics of neighbourhood or education or class but also in the process of what media expert John Fiske calls the 'exnomination' of whiteness as racial identity. Whiteness is unnamed, suppressed, beyond the realm of race. Exnomination permits whites to entertain the notion that race lives 'over there' on the other side of the tracks, in black bodies and inner-city neighbourhoods, in a dark netherworld where whites are not involved.

At this level, the creation of a sense of community is a life-long negotiation of endless subtlety. One morning when my son was three, I took him to his preschool. My son ran straight to a pile of Lego and proceeded to work. I crossed the room and put his lunchbox in the refrigerator, where I encountered a little girl sitting at a table, beating a mound of clay into submission with a plastic rolling pin. 'I see a Mommy,' she said to me cheerfully. 'That must mean that your little boy is here somewhere too.'

'Yes, he's here,' I answered, thinking how sweetly precocious she was. 'There, he's over by the Lego.'

She strained to see around the bookcases. 'Oh yes,' she said. 'Now I see that black face of his.'

I walked away without responding, enraged – how can one be so enraged at an innocent child – yet not knowing what to say just then, rushing to get the jaggedly dangerous broken glass of my emotions out of the room.

I remember being three years old so well. Three was the age when I learned that I was black, the coloured kid, monkeychild, different. What made me so angry and wordless in this encounter forty years later was the realisation that none of the little white children who taught me to see my blackness as a mark probably ever learned to see themselves as white. In our culture, whiteness is rarely marked in the indicative there! there! sense of my bracketed blackness. And the majoritarian privilege of never noticing oneself was the beginning of an imbalance from which so much, so much else flowed.

But that is hard to talk about, even now, this insight

acquired before I had the words to sort it out. Yet it is imperative to think about this phenomenon of closeting race, which I believe is a good deal more widespread than these small examples. In a sense, race matters are resented and repressed in much the same way as matters of sex and scandal: the subject is considered a rude and transgressive one in mixed company, a matter whose observation is sometimes inevitable, but about which, once seen, little should be heard none the less. Race thus tends to be treated as though it were an especially delicate category of social infirmity – so-called – like extreme obesity or disfigurement.

Every parent knows a little of this dynamic, if in other contexts: 'Why doesn't that lady have any teeth,' comes the child's piping voice. 'Why doesn't that gentleman have any hair?' And 'Why is that little boy so black?' *Sssshhhh!* comes the anxious parental remonstrance. The poor thing can't help it. We must all pretend that nothing's wrong.

And thus we are coached upon pain of punishment not to see a thing.

Now to be sure, the parent faces an ethical dilemma in that moment of childish vision unrestrained by social nicety. On the one hand, we rush to place a limit on what can be said to strangers and what must be withheld for fear of imposition or of hurting someone's feelings. As members of a broad society, we respect one another by learning not to inflict every last intimate, prying curiosity we may harbour upon everyone we meet.

That said, there remains the problem of how or whether we ever answer the question, and that is the dimension of this dynamic that is considerably more troubling.

'Why is that man wearing no clothes, Mummy?' pipes the childish voice once more. And the parent panics at the complication of trying to explain. The naked man may be a nudist or psychotic or perhaps the emperor of the realm, but the silencing that is passed from parent to child is not only about the teaching of restraint; it is calculated to circumnavigate the question as though it had never been asked. '*Stop asking such silly questions.*'

A wall begins to grow around the forbidden gaze; for we all know, and children best of all, when someone wants to change the subject, forever. And so the child is left to the monstrous creativity of ignorance and wild imagination.

Again, I do believe that this unfortunate negotiation of social difference has much in common with discussions about race. Race is treated as though it were some sort of genetic leprosy or a biological train wreck. Those who privilege themselves as Un-raced – usually but not always those who are white – are always anxiously maintaining that it doesn't matter even as they are quite busy feeling pity, no less, and thankful to God for their great good luck in having been spared so intolerable an affliction.

Meanwhile, those marked as Having Race are ground down by the pendular stresses of having to explain what it feels like to be You – why are you black, why are you black, why are you black, over and over again; or alternatively, placed in a kind of conversational quarantine of muteness in which any mention of racial circumstance reduces all sides to tears, fears, fisticuffs and other paroxyms of unseemly anguish.

This sad, habitual paralysis in the face of the foreign and the anxiety-producing. It is as though we are all skating across a pond that is not quite thoroughly frozen. Two centuries ago, or perhaps only a few decades ago, the lake was solidly frozen, and if for those skating across the surface things seemed much more secure, it was a much more dismal lot for those whose fates were frozen at the bottom of the pond. Over time, the weather of race relations has warmed somewhat, and a few of those at the bottom have found their way to the surface; we no longer hold our breath, and we have even learned to skate. The noisy, racial chasm still yawns darkly beneath us all, but we few brave souls glide gingerly above, upon a skim of hope, our bodies made light with denial, the black pond so dangerously and thinly iced with the conviction that talking about it will only make things worse.

And so the racial divide is exacerbated further by a welter of little lies that propels us foolishly around the edges of our most demanding social stresses: black people are a happy people and if they would just stop complaining so much, they would see how happy they are. Black people who say they're unhappy are leftist agitators whose time would be better spent looking for a real job. White people are victims. Poor Bangledeshis are poor because they want to be. Poor white people are poor because rich Indians stole all the jobs under the ruse of affirmative action. There is no racism in the market-place, 'each according to his merit' goes the cant, even as the Commission for Racial Equality receives 1700 formal complaints of racial discrimination every month; even as top executives funnel the jobs to school chums and their next of kin, or chief executives at major corporations are captured on tape destroying subpoenaed records of ongoing discriminatory practices. Immigrants are taking over the whole world, but race makes no difference. If sixty per cent of young black men are unemployed in the industrialised world, well, let them watch Oprah. If some people are determined to be homeless, well then let them have it, if homelessness is what they like so much. . .

'Triage' is a word I hear bandied about a lot these days. I have heard it used by many of my friends who are economists; they used it to convey an urgency of limited resources. If there's not enough to go around, then those with the least should be written off first because it will take more to save them anyway. And we don't have more.

This word *triage* originally cropped up in the context of the medical profession. It is a term borrowed from overtaxed hospitals in theatres of war. On body-strewn battefields, doctors would divide the survivors into three groups. The third in the worst condition might be left to die because bandages were better spent wrapped around those more likely to survive.

In the context of today's ghettos, inner cities and those places doomed to be called the Third World, I hear the word *triage*.

I worry about this image that casts aside so many so easily. It envisions poor and dying populations as separate, distant, severable. I worry that perhaps we have mis-chosen our metaphors.

I fear *triage*; I fear that one cannot cut off a third of the world without some awful, life-threatening bleeding in the rest of the body politic. The Malthusian nightmare has never been a simple matter, I think, of letting someone else go hungry, or of letting someone else die. It is a matter of amputation – that's the metaphor I'd rather use. And one can't cut off one's leg and pretend it never belonged.

It is as though we are employing, in our economic analysis of distributive justice, the images of the very earliest days of medical experimentation. *Oh, well, let's see now. . . The soul abides in the liver. . . therefore we can chop of that troublesome, heretical head and no one will be less holy for it. . .*

Maybe. But quite a few martyrs have been made that way.

Anthropologist Michael Taussig has written about the phenomenon of public secrets. He writes of a ritual in Tierra del Fuego in which the men come out of the men's hut wearing masks. The women hail them by singing 'Here come the spirits!' On some level, everyone must know that these are not spirits but husbands and brothers and fathers and sons, but so powerful is the ritual to the sense of community that it is upon pain of death that the women fail to greet them as spirits.

In our culture, I think that the power of race resembles just such a public secret. I understand the civic ritual that requires us to say in the face of all our differences, we are all one, we are the world. I understand the need for the publicly reiterated faith in public ideals as binding and sustaining community. Such beliefs are the very foundation of institutional legitimacy and no society can hold itself together without them. Yet such binding force comes from a citizenry willing to suspend disbelief for the sake of honouring the spiritual power of our appointed ideals. And where suspicion, cynicism and betrayal have eaten away at a community to the degree that the folk parading from the men's hut look like just a bunch of muggers wearing masks – or badges, as the case may be – then hailing the spirit will sound like a hollow incantation, empty theatre, the weary habit of the dispossessed.

There is a crisis of community in the United States no less than in the rest of the world, of specific and complicated origin perhaps, but in this moment of global upheaval, worth studying for possibilities both won and lost. Whites fear blacks, blacks fear whites. Each is the enemy against whom the authorities will not act.

If racial and ethnic experience constitute a divide that cannot be spoken, an even greater paradox is the degree to which a sense of commonality may be simultaneously created as well as threatened by notions of ethnicity and race. It is no wonder we end up deadlocked with so many of our most profound political problems. The 'O.J. divide' (as it's come to be known in America) is merely a convenient metaphor for everything else we disagree about. Are you one of 'us' or one of 'them'? When I say 'we' am I heard as referring only to other black people? When I employ the first person, will it only be heard as an exercise of what might be called the 'royal I' – me as representative stand-in for all those of my kind. . .

Certainly the great, philosophically-inspiring quandary of

my life is that despite the multiculturalism of my heritage and the profundity of my commitment to the notion of the 'us'-ness of us all, I have little room but to negotiate most of my daily lived encounters as one of 'them'. How alien this sounds. This split without, the split within.

Yet in this way the public secret of human fallibility, whose silence we keep to honour our symbolic civic unity, is vastly complicated by the counter secret of palpitating civil discord. Hail the spirit of our infallibly peaceful coexistence. Hail our common fate (even as young white men are forming their own private militias complete with grenade launchers and one in three young black men are in jail or on probation. . . But shush, don't stare. . .

Such is the legacy of racism in the modern world. Perhaps it is less and less fashionable these days to consider too explicitly the kinds of costs that slavery and colonialism exacted, even as those historical disruptions have continued to scar contemporary social arrangements with the transcendent urgency of their hand-me-down grief.

I realise therefore that it might be considered impertinent to keep raising the ghost of slavery's triangle trade and waving it around; there is a pronounced preference in polite society for just letting bygones be bygones. And I concede that a more optimistic enterprise might be to begin any contemporary analysis of race with the Civil Rights Movement in the United States, or the Notting Hill riots in the United Kingdom. Beginning at those points is a way of focusing one's view and confining one's reference to the legitimately inspiring ideals that coalesced those movements: the aims of colour-blindness, equality of all people, and the possibility of peaceful coexistence.

Yet if that well-chosen temporal slice allows us to be optimistic about the possibility of progress, there are none the less limitations to such a frame. First, it is the conceptual pre-history of those movements that explains the toll of racism and its lingering effects. There can be no adequate explanation without reference to it. Secondly, the diasporic complexity of today's social problems requires an analysis that moves those ideals of the social movements of the 1960s and 1970s beyond themselves, into the present, into the future – to a more complex, practical grappling with such phenomena as the hybridising of racial stereotypes with the fundamentalisms of gender, class, ethnicity, religion. Thirdly, the problem of race is overlaid with crises in environmental and resource management that have triggered unparalled migrations from rural to urban locations within national boundaries, and that have impassioned debates about immigration across national boundaries. Finally, not a few aspects of our new-age global economics, much like the commercial profiteering of colonialisms past, threaten to displace not just the very laws to which we persistently make such grand appeal but the nation state itself. I believe that a genuine, long-term optimism about the future of race relations depends on a thorough excavation of the same.

A memory slips into my mind. I was riding the train from New York to Washington DC some years ago. I was on my way to some lawyers' conference or other; I was accompanied by two black colleagues. An hour into the trip, the train stopped in the city of Philadelphia. A young white woman got on whom my colleagues knew. She was also a lawyer, headed to the same conference. She joined us, sitting among us in a double row of seats that faced each other. A little while later, the conductor came along. The new woman held up her ticket, but the conductor still came along. The new woman held up her ticket, but the conductor did not seem to see her. He saw four of us seated and only three ticket stubs.

'One of you hasn't paid,' he said, staring at me, then at each of my two black friends. I remember pointing to the

white woman and someone else said, 'Ove...
conductor was resolute.

'Which one of you hasn't paid?' he asked aga...
kept saying, 'Our receipts, see?' and the white wom...
ing *very* clearly said, 'Here. I am trying to give you m... ...et.'

The conductor was scowling. The conductor still did not
hear. 'I am not moving 'til one of you pays up.'

It was the longest time before the conductor stopped staring in all the wrong directions. It was the longest time before
he heard the new woman, pressing her ticket upon him, her
voice reaching him finally as though from a great distance,
passing through light years of understanding as though from
another universe. The realisation that finally lit his face was
like the dawning of a great surprise.

How precisely does the issue of colour remain so power-
fully determinative of everything from life circumstance to
manner of death, in a world that is, by and large, officially
'colour-blind'? What metaphors mask the hierarchies that
make racial domination frequently seem so 'natural', so invisible, indeed so attractive? How does racism continue to
evolve, post-slavery and post-equality legislation, across such
geographic, temporal and political distance?

No, I am not saying that this is the worst of times. But neither will I concede that this is the best of all possible worlds.
And what a *good* thing, is it not, to try to imagine how much
better we could be. . .

'I had a dream,' said my son the other morning. Then he
paused. 'No,' he said, 'it was more of a miracle. Do you know
what a miracle is?'

'Tell me,' I said, thunderstruck, and breathless with mater-
nal awe.

'A miracle is when you have a dream and you open your
eyes in it. It's when you wake up and your dream is all around
you.'

It was a pretty good definition, I thought. And even though

..y son's little miracle had something to do with pirates meeting dinosaurs, I do think that to a very great extent we dream our worlds into being. For better or worse, our customs and laws, our culture and society are sustained by the myths we embrace, the stories we recirculate to explain what we behold. I believe that racism's hardy persistence and immense adaptability are sustained by a habit of human imagination, deflective rhetoric and hidden license. I believe no less that an optimistic course might be charted, if only we could imagine it. What a world it would be if we could all wake up and see all of ourselves reflected in the world, not merely in a territorial sense, but with a kind of non-exclusive entitlement that grants not so much possession as investment. A peculiarly anachronistic notion of investment, I suppose, at once both ancient and futuristic. An investment that envisions each of us in each other.

2

The Pantomime of Race

If race is something about which we dare not speak in polite social company, the same cannot be said of the *viewing* of race. How, or whether, blacks are seen depends upon a dynamic of display that ricochets between hypervisibility and oblivion. Blacks are seen 'everywhere', taking over the world one minute; yet the great ongoing toll of poverty and isolation that engulfs so many remains the object of persistent oversight.

If, moreover, the real lives of real blacks unfold outside the view of many whites, the fantasy of black life as a theatrical enterprise is an almost obsessive indulgence. This sort of voyeurism is hardly peculiar to the mechanics of racial colonisation, of course: any group designated the colourful local, the bangled native or the folksy ethnic stands to suffer its peculiar limitation. But since it is racial voyeurism that has produced some of the biggest visual blockbusters of the century, one might as well begin there.

Consider, if you will indulge me for what I promise will be *just* a moment of exquisitely bad taste, the lurid babel that has been O.J. Simpson-mania. It might be a version, I suppose, of that great conversation about race we Americans are always telling ourselves we're going to have – albeit a conversation waged in a fan-danced pantomime of naked revelations followed by quick flutters of denial – words and images on completely different wavelengths, at constant war in a swirling mush of conflicting so-called 'information'.

Race! Sex! Miscegenation! screamed the front-page photos.

No Race, *No* Class. Just the American Way of Colour-blind Justice, demurely intoned so many of the sober wordsmiths and solemn television anchormen. Those who did talk about race, blacks by and large, were denounced grandly, not on substantive grounds, but for ever having imagined the subject into existence.

This scripted denial ultimately allowed visual images to remain in the realm of the unspoken, the unsaid filled by stereotypes and self-identifying illusion, the hierarchies of race and gender circulating unchallenged. This is the stuff of which obsession is formed.

I suppose I must say a little more about the Simpson phenomenon. There is perhaps no better example of the degree to which the cultural appetite for spicy brews of race, sex and crime has deployed 'real courts' to its own amusing little ends. But engaging as that drama became, so is it draining. It was certainly among the most exceptional spectacles in media history, and I am loathe to be one of those who would draw general lessons from a case that resembles nothing ever before seen on the planet earth. It provided no insight at all about what ordinary black, or white, defendants encounter in the criminal justice system, and yet it seems to me that the function of its obsessive hold was to create an imaginary window on what is *thought* to occur in the average courtroom to the average black defendant.

And that, I think, is the basis for so much of what chafes at the racial divide in discussions of this case. White people tended to imagine that this case was about hoards of guilty black defendants with sixteen lawyers going scot-free. And in trying to counter that impression, black people too tended to talk about Mr Simpson as though he were all black defendants.

While the bounds of fiction and non-fiction have always been blurred when it comes to our affection for a good whodunnit, the Simpson case became one long serial story, a chain novel with no threat of enduring social edification, a thicket of tragic possibilities and inexhaustible sub-plots, a graveyard of alternative theories ultimately decomposing toward sensory overload and infinity.

As an aside, I do think that if that trial provides a window into any kind of cultural meaning, we had better look to the way in which the panicky urgency of race overshadows the matter of class – that is, the contemporary license granted to the very wealthy or the very famous. While so many have blamed the acquittal upon the race of some of the jurors, it should not be forgotten that Americans have always been reticent to convict the very rich or the very famous. There has always been a certain conceptual overlap among the lavish forms of defense that wealth can buy, the transfixing aura of celebrity, and the golden glow of presumptive innocence.

But while we are so drenched in the passions of racial exorcism attending the Simpson case, it is instructive to take a quick peek into the courtrooms where the dramas of two other wealthy former sports heroes have unfolded rather more quietly. Mr Alex Kelly, a young white athlete accused of raping a high-school classmate, fled the United States and with the financial assistance of his well-to-do parents, lived lavishly abroad, hopping from one European ski resort to another, for ten years before he was found. His trial ended in a hung jury despite eyewitnesses and lots of blood-stained evidence. The jury was – gasp! – all white. Would it reveal much, I wonder, to bewail this outcome as showing how supposedly 'partial' white people are in judging one of 'their own'.

Similarly, we might consider Mr John DuPont, heir to the massive DuPont fortune, who for years drove around his up-market neighbourhood in an armoured tank bristling with sophisticated weaponry, with the full knowledge of local authorities I might add; Mr John DuPont who, in the presence of witnesses, shot and killed an Olympic wrestling champion living on the grounds of his estate. If we wish to obsess about the vagaries of our justice system, this seems as fair a case as any. What irony, when we last heard from the DuPont family it was from his brother, Mr Pete DuPont, who was quoted in *The National Review* saying that 'The minimum wage turns out to be one of our leading killers. . . It's time to stop it before it kills again.'[1] In fact if we really wanted equality of legal circus, perhaps we should have round-the-clock coverage of either of the Messieurs DuPont walking toward the courthouse, in slow motion, while a little Greek chorus of black experts chanted lamentations about how white people have corrupted the moral fibre of our civilisation. Is it any less absurd to think of O.J. Simpson as representative of the morals of all black people than to judge all white people by the murderous belligerence of a John DuPont?

I offer these rather crude reversals because perhaps they highlight this peculiarly pornographic *seeing* of race in the Simpson case: the nearsighted unblinking focused gaze that in the United States was signalled by the television networks cancelling coverage of the first World Cup to be held in the US, so that helicopter cameras could train spotlights upon Mr Simpson's flight from the police; or that was signalled by *Time Magazine*'s cover photo of Mr Simpson with his skin airbrushed darker so as to achieve what they seemed to think was a certain demonic drama. This staging of the case as an 'event' from the very beginning was no less a 'playing of the race card' than when, months later, defence attorneys spoke race aloud, introducing tapes of the infamous racist rantings of Detective Mark Furhman, who was later convicted of perjury.

1 Pete Dupont, 'Pay Hazard', *The National Review*, 1 May 1995, p. 74.

I bother to mention any of this because I long ago discarded the notion that the Simpson case was merely a contained domestic embarrassment. I have found myself called to account for this bizarre spectacle by taxi drivers in London, friends in France, tourists from Turkey. A Chinese–American student of mine, describing her most recent visit to family in Hong Kong, found that her most memorable encounter was in a McDonald's restaurant where a big-screen television had been installed, and crowds of Hong Kong teenagers sat soberly ingesting Big Macs, french fries, and that day's slow motion replays of the Trial of the Century.

Does voyeurism even begin to capture the intensity of this cultural moment – this ultimate test of the bounds between fact and fiction, fiction and fixation, fixation and the religious fervour of an outright passion play.

In any case, for all the spectacularly lurid razzle of the Simpson case, there are quieter instances of racial voyeurism that are perhaps at least as telling. For example: in black neighbourhoods around the United States, but most particularly in well-known communities like Harlem and New York, busloads of tourists flock to black churches on a Sunday morning, or any other time for that matter, gate-crashing baptisms and choir practice, prayer groups and funerals. The *New York Times* covered the event not long ago – caravans of Swedes and Japanese and Dutch and Brazilians, fighting with congregants for good seats, straining for the perfect camera angles, hunkering down for a good show. It's great theatre, according to the guidebook list of hits, all those black people dressed in their quaint finery, singing and swooning and singing some more. (In order to understand fully the impact of such an event, it might help to imagine a village church in a small homogenous locale in Middle England. I imagine that four hundred of, oh, say, me, four hundred Americans, four hundred black people, either or both, take your pick show up, outnumbering the congregation, well-meaning surely, except perhaps for the chewing gum, the flashbulbs and those Bruce Springsteen T-shirts.)

I first encountered this event some years ago, when I went on a walking tour of Harlem, supposedly to view the architectural idiosyncrasies of the neighbourhood. The guide proposed quite casually that we drop in on some churches to 'see the show'. There was a meandering quality to the suggestion, we could go here, we could go there. We could look at the marble detailing a block north, we could look at the people praying a block south. The people praying were on a par with the marble detailing – there for the observation. There was no thought of invitation or interaction, no fear of transgression. A presumption of right to be there, if anything, for when I objected that it didn't seem appropriate to treat a congregation as just another monument, I was told that 'no one would mind'. I took it to mean that no one they felt obligated to listen to had told them they would mind.

I could not help thinking of property accounts taken during the times of slavery, in which slaves were listed along with the furniture. Two beds, four armchairs, one mahogany armoir, three antimacassars, one parlour maid. . .

There's a long tradition of religion being the window through which culture is observed and learned. But there is also a long tradition of voyeurism as a means of putting culture not just on display but at a condescending distance. (I think of an old photograph I once saw, taken in the south of the United States shortly after the Civil War, in which a family of white landowners were arranged upon a grassy bluff, enjoying an elegant picnic spread. As they ate, they watched a black congregation engaged in the ritual of baptism in the river below.)

My father, who grew up in the segregated south recalls this phenomenon even as he was growing up: whites would come for the thrill of the purportedly boisterous carryings-on in black churches. He describes how it would inhibit the sense of communion, of joy and release, this one-way gaze of the soberly disengaged, in whose world you would never be permitted the intimacy of such study. In deference to the unbidden visitors, the congregations would strain for greater 'decorum' so as not to be the objects of anything that felt like mockery, that felt like ridicule.

But what makes a church a house of God is a question of faith. What transports those who form a congregation to the shared catharsis that is holy communion is the willingness to suspend disbelief. Imagine how hard it is to maintain that sense of intimacy and vulnerability when four hundred tourists show up, late, and stay long enough to hear three rousing gospel songs but not so long as to endanger lunch reservations at the South Street Seaport. Imagine that they all get up during the children's offering and, four-hundred strong, crash their way toward the exits. Imagine how hard to it is to hear above that din the warbly little voices of the children, so young, so brave and so insulted; imagine how hard it becomes to suspend cynicism – never mind disbelief. The cost of continuing in this path is that people grow apart rather than closer. The churches lose not only their sense of community, but respect for the tourist. This drives people to draw boundaries where none ought to be.

I would ask you to imagine, too, how hard it is to draw any kind of boundary around a house of worship. How do you distinguish at the door the spiritual seeker from the thrill-seeker? Indeed those churches that have expressed their unwillingness to continue to 'entertain' tour groups still receive as many as two hundred individually-motivated tourists, in some instances, on any given Sunday. Moreover, those same churches, having attempted to impose some sorts of limits on attendance and decorum, have faced charges of being racist, separatist, nationalist, and of course that great all-time favourite, politically correct.

It is a dilemma surely. For the extrication from such tension relies upon the restraint of the tourist, of the anthropological instinct that lends such sense of entitlement to the project of studying those whose willingness to be studied is assumed as given. In the grip of such blissful entitlement, what a surprise the eruption of anti-colonial fundamentalism! What a shock! How irrational! And after all we've done for them, paying good money to come see them and the nostalgia of their charming culture. . .

Meanwhile, on the other side of the fence, consider the seductive temptations of other dangerous rationales – for when we are pushed to the limit, forced to the insistence on boundary – this is a step toward fundamentalism. For what is fundamentalism in its most inchoate sense but the felt necessity for a hard bright line between those who are 'true' believers and those others, those infidels who are known for their transgression.

While the interest in black churches may be good, may be welcome in many senses, I worry that in important ways it signals the practice of *dis*interest. One Sunday, for example, I rather boldly asked a young French tourist whether she had thought about having worn tennis shorts to a church.

'But we're going to play tennis afterwards,' she replied with a fetching little pout of astonishment that implied I had said something quite stupid indeed. What on earth was I suggesting, wearing a dress to play tennis! When I drooped visibly at this response, she grew somewhat abashed. 'But everyone goes dressed like this,' she said. By everyone she apparently meant other French tourists. Everybody did not mean me; it did not include the congregants.

She went on to rationalise the tennis togs with a fine display of the craft of projecting one's own self-interest on to the world at large: 'They are mostly very poor people anyway,' again apparently exceptionalising me. 'There are a lot of homeless people who attend. *They'd* be uncomfortable if we did get dressed up.'

Such is the prattle of the invested voyeur. Such is the happily insular comfort of the safari adventure, the ambling browse through the living museum, the stalking of wild life forms, the thrill of capturing authentic natural phenomena, the safe rapture yet the distant danger of coming so close to the Lost Link, the primitive origins of some more innocent beginning. And so the pilgrimage to the tribal enclosure, cameras in hand, the image, if not exactly stuffed, rendered two dimensional. The flat, dry, matted photographic relic to be spread out upon the coffee tables of faraway homes; the open-mouthed exotics, frozen in raucous song, glazed in a bath of light from the high-beamed cameras; the startled prey bagged with the click of a blazing hot flashbulb.

Like tigers, I would guess, real untethered blacks would never be invited into these homes of the hunter. Maybe someone who had the room for a menagerie, but for the average tourist, well, bringing home such a prize is simply too expensive, and besides the neighbours might complain.

Alas, am I too cynical? Let me ask the question more straightforwardly. Is it really the experience of religious communion that is retained by all these camera-toting tourists? It is my fear that for all the stated aspiration, it is not an appreciation of black culture that is carried away on film and tape but an appropriation, and a shallow one at that. I am thinking of an Hawaiian friend of mine who went to college on the mainland, who described her sense of confusion upon attending a fraternity party with a so-called Hawaiian 'theme'. Random cultural objects were thrown about the room, with no rhyme or reason; it took her a long time to realise that there was no rhyme or reason. The things just looked Hawaiian. Nothing more.

I think a factor of major importance in all this is one's relation to images of the alluring and the bestial, of civilisation and the savage. Cultural domination of any sort and most particularly racial domination is facilitated by powerful erotic archetypes in which deep prejudices are 'felt' rather than reasoned, and thereby naturalised rather than beheld. These archetypes, or stereotypes, so control the limits of imagination that even conscious attempts to explore 'the foreign other' become rather too easily derailed: the quest to embrace cultures other than one's own degenerate into a taste for the 'fauve' and the 'primitive' – fiercely co-optive rather than appreciative of other worlds.

There are always, I suppose, a few exotics who may be admitted to the inner circle, those well-paid few who teach the upper classes how to dance that dance and paint that paint. But too often and too soon the circle closes back upon itself, congratulating itself for its mastery of the foreign, always preferring familiar drama to the risks of serious democratisation. This erotic boundary between the desired and the undesirable, forming such an insistently closed circle of self-regard, nevertheless offers itself up as universal; the created prison of expectation never quite permitting the shock of intimate surprise, never a glimpse into the realm of the unknown, the unprepossessed, the unprejudiced.

Let me try to make this point with a somewhat different emphasis, restated, again, as an ethical challenge. Philosophers from Aristotle to Hannah Arendt have spoken of the condition of 'being one'. In its most literal sense, the ability to be one person rather than two refers to some resolution of the ethically dangerous position of one who finds oneself split between the one one is, and the one one feels one *has* to be. The sheltered self and the masquerade.

A black lawyer friend of mine describes a situation that I think exemplifies this split: when her firm first hired her, all the new associates were taken to lunch at an exclusive private club that had until only shortly before barred blacks, Jews and women as members. She found herself the only black person seated at the table while all the servers were black. She found herself on what she called a 'razor's edge' of social conscious-ness – she was supposed to be enjoying the fruits of her professional success; she was, she knew, supposed to display some subtle mixture of wit, grace and gratitude. Yet sitting at that table engaged in conversation about corporate mergers while acknowledging 'the help' only by the quiet sway of her body from right to left as the plates came and went, felt to her like 'ignoring my family,' as she put it.

To review the ingredients thus far: for black people, the sys-temic, often nonsensical denial of racial experiences engenders a sense of split identity attending that which is obvious but inexpressible; an assimilative tyranny of neutral-ity as self-erasure. It creates an environment in which one cannot escape the clanging symbolism of oneself. This is heightened by contrast to all the silent, shifty discomfort of suffering condescension. There's that clunky social *box*, larger than your body, taking up all that space. You need two chairs at the table, one for you, one for your blackness.

For white people, moreover, racial denial tends to engen-der a profoundly invested disingenuousness, an innocence that amounts to the transgressive refusal to know. Again, this is not to assign anything like blame, simply to observe the way in which we know race, or don't. In the wake of that club luncheon, for example, my lawyer friend mentioned her sense of distress at the social imbalance of the event to one of her colleagues. She was instantly suffused with apolo-gies. Neither my friend nor I is so cynical to doubt her sincerity. Yet both of us confessed to a weariness with such apologies. Both of us had been in so very many situations where white people just didn't *know*, had just never *thought* about it.

At some point the flow of apologies begins to feel like a gulf of false empathy. At some point a suspicion sets in of the wistful giftiness with which not-knowing is offered. The grand admission of vulnerability that is an invitation to more work for you. 'Do tell me all about it!' The guilty childishness that never *dreamed* of such a thing: 'How awful it must be for you! And how terrible I feel now that I know!' All the while, a kind of pleading behind the eyes, a twisting of nervously clutched hankies – and the anxious call to colour-blindness: *Would that you would just not-know too.*

Again, I do not want to disparage the sincerity of such conversations, only their superficiality and the troublesomeness of that reiterated emptiness. How can it be that so many well-meaning white people have never thought about race when so few blacks pass a single day without being reminded of it? How is it that the very suggestion that white people think about it is considered a bad or a burdensome thing, as though there could never be good and constructive insights from it, as though the excitation of too much thought about race could drive one howling into the abyss. Better just to pluck out one's eyeballs, I suppose.

So it is not merely the silence about racism that presents problems, but its aesthetic *visual* power as well. Thus I believe that racial representations in popular culture present a most urgent concern in a society as relentlessly bombarded with visual images as ours. Visual symbolism has begun to rival spoken or printed words as the medium by which our sense of cultural tradition is to be carried forward.

The globally pervasive manipulation of the vocabulary of visual images is why I think that talking out our differences, or 'conversation' by itself cannot begin to be adequate. It can't work, in this age of television and film, if, for example, we proceed to converse about 'crime', say, our words neutral as can be – yet at some deep, collectively unconscious level, we share a vision of a black but not a white criminal, or vice versa. Or if one of us has determined to avenge not victims in some general sense, but victims only of a particular race. Or gender. Or religion.

It is a tribute to the power of television, perhaps, that the very tiny minority of black and Asian people in Great Britain – five per cent – is the focus of such immense anxiety to so many in the remaining ninety-five per cent. The dimension of race, the proportion of race, the numbers of race become inflated, exaggerated, distorted, enlarged. Five per cent becomes one thousand per cent in the infinitely multiplying, endlessly replayed hallucinations of the television hall of mirrors. It is in this way, perhaps, that the project of inclusion is felt as one of takeover; that the goal of equality comes to be seen as favouritism; that the travails of so few become the scapegoat for so many.

In order to make sense of our cyclical racial passion plays, in other words, we need to pull together a comprehensive analysis of words and images, in both high and low culture, in both major and minor traditions of literature, sociology and law. Why can we not speak of race but only mutter and groan? Why can we not look at the problem but only peer at it with the overcharged currents of pornography? Examining the extent to which the stakes in whiteness impassion so many of our race rituals may be one way of reclaiming a coherent connection between our free-floating mythological fears and their consequence – the actual data of racial anxiety, division and violence.

My compatriot Henry Louis Gates wrote an intriguing piece in the *New Yorker* magazine not long ago. It was about Anatole Broyard, a light-skinned black man who passed as a white man for most of his adult life. Since Broyard was well-known in the United States as an editor of the *New York Times Book Review*, it came as a rude shock to many when Gates' article revealed 'the truth'. I suppose that this case could be an example of the assimilative pressures that so conspire to create a more sophisticated version of what I call the Michael Jackson syndrome of self-elimination. But Gates raises a harder conundrum posed by Broyard's situation: 'Anatole

Broyard wanted to be a writer, not a black writer. So he chose to live a lie rather than be trapped by the truth.'

Where is the space, I wonder, between the lived lie and the trap of the truth? What do we look like when we try to inhabit the shades of grey? Are we driven beyond ourselves when we set out just to be ourselves? Black or white, invisible or conspicuous, English or British, raced or nationed, embodied or alone. . . Who are we when we are seen but not spotlighted, when we are humble but not invisible, when we matter but not so much that the mattering drives us mad.

3

The Distribution of Distress

Many years ago, I was standing in a so-called juice bar in Berkeley, California. A young man came in whom I had often seen begging in the neighbourhood. A more bruised-looking human one could not imagine: he was missing several teeth, his clothes were in rags, his blond hair was matted, his eyes red-rimmed, his nails long and black and broken. On this particular morning he came into the juice bar and ordered some sort of protein drink from the well-scrubbed, patchouli-scented young woman behind the counter. It was obvious that his presence disturbed her, and when he took his drink and mumbled, 'Thanks, little lady,' she exploded.

'Don't you dare call me "little lady"!' she snarled with a ferocity that turned heads. 'I'm a *woman* and you'd better learn the difference!'

'Sorry,' he whispered with his head bowed, like a dog that had been kicked, and he quite literally limped out of the store.

'Good riddance,' the woman called after him.

This took place some fifteen years ago, but I have always remembered the interchange because it taught me a lot about the not-so-subliminal messages that can be wrapped in the expression of Virtue Aggrieved, in which anti-bias of one sort is used to further the agenda of bias of another kind.

In an abstract sense, I understood the resentment of girlish diminutives. Too often as a lawyer I have been in courtroom situations where coy terms of endearment were employed in such a way that 'the little lady, God-Bless-Her,' became a marginalising condescension, a precise condensation of 'She thinks she's a lawyer, poor thing.' Yet in this instance, gender power was clearly not the issue, but rather the emotional venting of a revulsion at this man's dirty and bedraggled presence. It wasn't just that he had called her a little lady; she seemed angry that he had dared address her at all.

If, upon occasion, the ploughshare of feminism can be beaten into a sword of class prejudice, no less can there be other examples of what I call battling biases, in which the impulse to anti-discrimination is defeated by the intrusion or substitution of a different object of enmity. This revolving door of revulsions is one of the trickiest mechanisms contributing to the enduring nature of prejudice; it is at heart, I suppose, a kind of traumatic reiteration of injurious encounters, preserving even as it transforms the overall history of rage.

I was in England several years ago when a young Asian man was severely beaten in East London by a young white man. I was gratified to see the immediate renunciation of racism that ensued in the media. It was a somewhat more sophisticated and heartfelt collective self-examination than sometimes occurs in the United States in the wake of such incidents, where, I fear, we are much more jaded about all forms of violence. Nevertheless, what intrigued me most about the media coverage of this assault was the unfortunate way in which class bias became a tool for the denunciation of racism.

'Racial, ethnic or religious prejudice is repugnant,' screamed the headlines.

Hooray, I thought.

And then the full text: 'It is repugnant, *particularly*', and I'm embellishing here, 'when committed by a miserable low-class cockney whose bestial nature knows no plummeted depth, etc. etc.'

Oh dear, I thought.

In other words, the media not only defined anti-Asian and anti-immigrant animus as ignorance, as surely it is, but went on to define that ignorance as the property of a class, of 'the' lower classes, implying even that a good Oxbridge education inevitably lifts one above that sort of thing. As surely it does not.

And therein lies a problem, I think. If race or ethnicity is not a synonym for either ignorance or foreignness, then neither should class be an explanatory trashbin for racial prejudice, domestic incivility and a host of other social ills. If the last fifty years have taught us nothing else, it is that our 'isms' are no less insidious when beautifully polished and terribly refined.

None of us is beyond some such pitfalls and in certain contexts, typecasting can even be a necessary and helpful way of explaining the social world. The hard task is to untangle the instances where the categoric helps us predict and prepare for the world from those instances where it verges into scapegoating, projection and prejudice.

To restate the problem, I think that the persistance of racism, ethnic and religious intolerance, as well as gender and class bias are dependant upon recirculating images in which the general and the particular duel each other endlessly.

'*En garde*, you heathenish son of an inferior category!'

'Brute!' comes the response. 'I am inalienably endowed with the unique luminosity of my rational individualism; it is you who are the gutteral eruption of an unspeakable sub-classification. . .'

Thrust and parry, on and on, the play of race versus ethnicity versus class versus blood feud. One sword may be sharper or quicker, but neither's wound is ever healed.

Too often these tensions are resolved simply by concluding that stereotyping is just our lot as humans so let the consequences fall where they may. But stereotyping operates as habit not immutable trait, a fluid project that rather too easily flows across the shifting ecology of human relations. And racism is a very old, very bad habit.

This malleability of prejudice is underscored by a little cultural comparison. If class bias has skewed discussions of racism in the British examples I have just described, it is rather more common in the United States for race to consume discussions of class altogether. While I don't want to overstate the cultural differences between the United States and the United Kingdom – there is enough similarity to conclude that race and class present a generally interlocking set of problems in both nations – the United States does deem itself classless with almost the same degree of self-congratulation that the United Kingdom prides itself on being largely free of a history of racial bias. Certainly these are good impulses, and desirable civic sentiments, but I am always one to look closely at what is deemed beyond the pale. *It will never happen here*. . . The noblest denials are at least as interesting study as the highest ideals.

Consider: for a supposedly classless society, the United States nevertheless suffers the greatest gap of any industrialised nation between its richest and poorest citizens. And there can be no more dramatic and ironic class consciousness than the Dickensian characteristics ascribed to those in the so-called 'underclass', as opposed to the rest – what are we to call them, the *over*class? Those who are deemed to have class versus those who are so far beneath the usual indicia of even lower class that they are deemed to have no class at all.

If this is not viewed by most Americans as a problem of class stasis, it is perhaps because class denominations are so uniformly understood to be stand-ins for race. The very term underclass is a *euphemism* for blackness, class operating as euphemism in that we Americans are an upbeat kind of people and class is usually thought to be an easier problem than race.

Middleclassness, on the other hand, is so persistently a euphemism for whiteness, that middle-class black people are sometimes described as 'honourary whites' or as those who have been deracinated in some vaguely political sense. More often than I like to remember, I have been told that my opinion about this or that couldn't possibly be relevant to 'real', 'authentic' black people, why? Simply because I don't sound like a Hollywood stereotype of the way black people are 'supposed' to talk. 'Speaking white' or 'Talking black'. No in-between. Speaking as a black person while sounding like a white person has, I have found, engendered some complicated sense of betrayal. '*You're* not black! You're not *white*!' No one seems particularly interested in the substantive ideas being expressed; but everyone is caught up with the question of whether anyone should have to listen to a white-voiced black person.

It is in this way that we often talk about class and race such that we sometimes end up talking about neither, because we insist on talking about race as though it were class and class as though it were race and it's hard to see very clearly when the waters are so muddied with all that simile and metaphor.

By the same token, America is usually deemed a society in which the accent with which one speaks Does Not Matter. That is largely true, but it is not so where black accents are concerned. While there is much made of regional variations – New Yorkers, Minnesotans and Southerners are the butts of a certain level of cheap satire – an accent deemed 'black' is the one with some substantial risk of evoking outright discrimination. In fact, the speech of real black people ranges from true dialects to myriad patois, to regional accents, to specific syntactical twists or usages of vocabulary. Yet language identified as black is habitually flattened into some singularised entity that in turn becomes synonymous with ignorance, slang, big lips and sloppy tongues, incoherent ideas, and very bad – terribly unruly! – linguistic acts. Black speech becomes a cipher for all the other stereotypes associated with racial discrimination; the refusal to understand becomes rationalised by the assumption of incomprehensibility.

My colleague, Professor Mari Matsuda has studied cases involving accent discrimination. She writes of lawsuits whose transcripts revealed an interesting paradox. One case featured a speaker whose accent had been declared incomprehensible by his employer. Nevertheless, his recorded testimony, copied down with no difficulty by the court reporter, revealed a parlance more grammatically accurate, substantively coherent, and syntactically graceful than any other speaker in the courtroom, including the judge. This paradox has always been the subject of some interest among linguists and sociolinguists, the degree to which language is understood in a way that is intimately linked to relations among speakers.

'Good day,' I say to you. Do you see me as a genial neighbour, as part of your day? If so, you may be generously disposed to return the geniality with a hearty 'Hale fellow, well met.'

'Good day,' I say. Do you see me as an impudent upstart the very sound of whose voice is an unwelcome intrusion upon your good day. If so, the greeting becomes an act of aggression; woe betide the cheerful, innocent upstart.

'Shall we consider race?' I say to you. If you are disposed

to like me you might hear this as an invitation to a kind of conversation we have not shared before, a leap of faith into knowing more about each other.

'Shall we consider race?' I say. *Not* 'Shall I batter you with guilt before we riot in the streets?' But only: 'Shall we *consider* race?' Yet if I am that same upstart, the blood will have boiled up in your ears by now, and very shortly you will start to have tremors at the unreasonable audacity of my meddlesome presumption. Nothing I actually say will matter for what matters is that I am out of place. . .

This dynamic, this vital ingredient of the willingness to hear is apparent in the contradiction of lower-status speech being simultaneously understood yet not understood. Why is the sound of black voices, the shape of black bodies so overwhelmingly agreeable, so colourfully comprehensible in some contexts, particularly in the sports and entertainment industries, yet deemed so utterly incapable of effective communication or acceptable presence when it comes to finding a job as a construction worker?

This is an odd conundrum, to find the sight and the sound of oneself a red flag. And it is a kind of banner, one's face and one's tongue, a banner of family and affiliation – that rhythm and stress, the bouyance of one's mother's tongue; that plane of jaw, that prominence of brow, the property of one's father's face. What to make of those social pressures that would push the region of the body underground in order to allow the purity of one's inner soul to be more fully seen. When Martin Luther King urged that we be judged by the content of our character surely he meant that what we looked like should not matter. Yet just as surely that enterprise did not involve having to deny the entirely complicated symbolic character of one's physical manifestation. This is a hard point, I confess, and one fraught with risk of misunderstanding. The colour of one's skin is a part of ourselves. It does not matter. It is precious, and yet it should not matter; it is important and yet it must not matter. It is simultaneously our greatest vanity and anxiety, and I am of the opinion, like Martin Luther King, that none of this should matter.

Yet let me consider the question of self-erasure. I've written elsewhere about my concern that various forms of biotechnological engineering have been turned to such purposes – from skin lighteners to cosmetic surgery to the market for sperm with blond hair and eggs with high IQs. Consider the little boy I read about who had started some sort of computer magazine for children. A young boy of eleven, celebrated as a computer whiz. A little boy whose family had emigrated from Puerto Rico, now living in New York. The article recounted how much he loved computers because, he said, nobody judged him for what he looked like, and he could speak without an accent. What to make of this freedom as disembodiment, this technologically-purified mental communion as escape from the society of others, as neutralised social space. What a delicate project, this looking at each other, seeing yet not staring. Would we look so hard, judge so hard, be so hard – what would we look like? – if we existed unselfconsciously in our bodies – sagging, grey-haired, young, old, black, white, balding and content?

Let me offer a more layered illustration of the way in which these issues of race and class interact, the markers of class distinction and bias in the United Kingdom emerging also in the United States as overlapping substantially with the category of race. A few years ago, I purchased a house. Because the house was in a different state than where I was located at the time, I obtained my mortgage by telephone. I am a prudent little squirrel when it comes to things financial, always tucking away sufficient stores of nuts for the winter, and so I meet the criteria of a quite good credit risk. My loan was approved almost immediately.

A short time after, the contract came in the mail. Among the papers the bank forwarded were forms documenting compliance with what is called the Fair Housing Act. It is against the law to discriminate against black people in the housing market, and one of the pieces of legislation to that effect is the Fair Housing Act, a law that monitors lending practices to prevent banks from doing what is called 'red-lining'. Red-lining is a phenomenon whereby banks circle certain neighbourhoods on the map and refuse to lend in those areas for reasons based on race. There are a number of variations on the theme. Black people cannot get loans to purchase homes in white areas; or black people cannot get startup money for small businesses in black areas. The Fair Housing Act thus tracks the race of all banking customers to prevent such discrimination. Unfortunately, some banks also use the racial information disclosed on the Fair Housing forms to engage in precisely the discrimination the law seeks to prevent.

I should repeat that to this point that my entire mortgage transaction had been conducted by telephone. I should also say that I speak what is considered in the States a very Received-Standard-English, regionally northeastern perhaps, but not marked as black. With my credit history, with my job as a law professor, and no doubt with my accent, I am not only middle class, but match the cultural stereotype of a good white person. It is thus perhaps that the loan officer of this bank, whom I had never met in person, had checked off a box on the Fair Housing form indicating that I *was* 'white'.

Race shouldn't matter, I suppose, but it seemed to in this case and so I took a deep breath, crossed out 'white', checked the box marked 'black' and sent the contract back to the bank. That will teach them to presume too much, I thought. A done deal, I assumed.

Suddenly said deal came to a screeching halt. The bank wanted more money as a down payment, they wanted me to pay more 'points' as certain extra charges are called, they wanted to raise the rate of interest. Suddenly I found myself facing great resistance and much more debt.

What was most interesting about all this was that the reason the bank gave for its new-found recalcitrance was not race, heaven forbid – racism doesn't exist anymore, hadn't I heard? No, the reason they gave was that property values in that neighbourhood were suddenly falling. They wanted more money to cover the increased risk.

Initially, I was surprised, confused. The house was in a neighbourhood that was extremely stable; prices in the area had not gone down since World War II, only slowly, steadily up. I am an extremely careful shopper and I had uncovered absolutely no indication that prices were falling at all.

It took my estate agent to make me see the light. 'Don't you get it,' he sighed. 'This is what they always do.'

And even though I work with this sort of thing all the time, I really hadn't gotten it: for of course, *I* was the reason the prices were in peril.

The bank was proceeding according to demographic data that show any time black people move into a neighbourhood in the States, whites are overwhelmingly likely to move out. In droves. In panic. In concert. Pulling every imaginable resource with them, from school funding to garbage collection to social workers who don't want to work in black neighbourhoods to police whose too-frequent relation to black communities is a corrupted one of containment rather than protection.

It's called a tipping point, this thing that happens when black people move into white neighbourhoods. The imagery is awfully catchy you must admit: the neighbourhood just tipping right on over like a terrible accident, whoops! Like a pitcher I suppose. All that nice fresh wholesome milk spilling out, running away. . . leaving the dark, echoing, upended urn of the inner city.

This immense fear of 'the black' next door is one reason the United States is so densely segregated. Only two per cent of white people have a black neighbour, even though black people comprise approximately 13 per cent of the population. White people fear black people in big ways, in small ways, in financial ways, in utterly incomprehensible ways.

As for my mortgage, I threatened to sue and eventually procured the loan on the original terms. But what was fascinating to me about this whole incident was the way in which this so exemplified the new problems of the new rhetoric of racism. For starters, the new rhetoric of racism never mentions race. It wasn't race but risk with which the bank was concerned. Secondly, since financial risk is all about economics, my exclusion got reclassified as just a consideration of class and there's no law against class discrimination, after all, for that would present a restraint on one of our most precious liberties, the freedom to contract or not. If public schools, trains, buses, swimming pools and neighbourhoods remain segregated it's no longer a racial problem if someone who just happens to be white keeps hiking the price for someone who just accidentally and purely by the way happens to be black. White people set higher prices for the 'right', the 'choice' of self-segregation. If black people don't move in it's just that they can't *afford* to. Black people pay higher prices for the attempt to integrate, even as the integration of oneself is a threat to one's investment by lowering its value.

By this measure of mortgage-worthiness, the ingredient of blackness is cast not just as a social toll but an actual tax. A fee, an extra contribution at the door, an admission charge for the higher costs of handling my dangerous propensities, my inherently unsavoury properties. I was not judged based on my independent attributes or individual financial worth as a client; nor even was I judged by statistical profiles of what my group actually do. (For in fact anxiety-stricken, middle-class, black people make grovellingly good cake-baking neighbours when not made to feel defensive by the unfortunate, historical, welcome strategies of bombs, burnings or abandon.)

Rather, I was being evaluated based on what an abstraction of White Society writ large thinks we – or I – do, and that imagined 'doing' was treated and thus established as a self-fulfilling prophecy.

However rationalised, this form of discrimination is a burden: one's very existence becomes a lonely vacuum when so many in society not only devalue *me*, but devalue *themselves* and their homes for having me as part of the landscaped view from the quiet of their breakfast nook.

I know, I know, I exist in the world on my own terms surely. I am an individual and all that. But if I carry the bank's logic out with my individuality rather than my collectively imagined effect on property values as the subject of this type of irrational economic computation, then *I*, the charming and delightful Patricia J. Williams, become a bit like a carwash in your backyard. Only much worse in real price terms. I am more than a mere violation of the nice residential comfort-zone in question; my blackness can re-zone altogether by the mere fortuity of my relocation.

'Dumping district', cringes the nice, clean, actuarial family-next-door. 'There goes the neighbourhood. . .' as whole geographic tracts slide into the chasm of impecuniousness and disgust. I am the economic equivalent of a medical waste disposal site, a toxic heap-o'-home.

In my brand new house, I hover behind my brand new kitchen curtains, wondering whether the very appearance of my self will endanger my collateral yet further. When Benneton ran an advertisement that darkened Queen Elizabeth II's skin to a nice rich brown, *The Sun* newspaper ran an article observing that this 'obviously cheapens the monarchy.' Will the presentation of my self so disperse the value of my own, my ownership, my property?

This is madness, I am sure, as I draw the curtain like a veil across my nose. In what order of things is it *rational* to thus hide and skulk?

It is an intolerable logic. An investment in my property compels a selling of myself.

I grew up in a white neighbourhood where my mother's family had been the only black people for about fifty years. In the 1960s, Boston began to feel the effects of the great migration of southern blacks to the north that came about as a result of the Civil Rights Movement. Two more black families moved into the neighbourhood. There was a sudden churning, a chemical response, a collective roiling with streams of froth and jets of steam. We children heard all about it on the playground. The neighbourhood was under seige. The blacks were coming. My schoolmates' parents were moving out *en masse*.

It was remarkable. The neighbourhood was entirely black within about a year.

I am a risk pool. I am a carwash.

I was affected, I suppose, growing up with those children who frightened themselves by imagining what it would be like to touch black bodies, to kiss those wide unkissable lips, to draw the pure breath of life through that crude and forbidden expanse of nose; is it really possible that a gentle God – their God, dear God – would let a *human* heart reside within the wet charred thickness of black skin?

I am, they told me, a jumble of discarded parts: low-browed monkey bones and infected, softly pungent flesh.

In fact, my price on the market is a variable affair. If I were crushed and sorted into common elements, my salt and juice and calcinated bits are worth approximately five English pounds. Fresh from the kill, in contrast, my body parts, my lungs and liver, heart and healthy arteries would fetch some forty thousand. There is no demand for the fruit of my womb, however; eggs fresh from its warm dark sanctuary are worthless on the open market. 'Irish Egg Donor Sought', reads an ad in the little weekly newspaper that serves New York City's parent population. And in the weird economy of bloodlines, and with the insidious variability of prejudice, 'Irish eggs' command a price of upwards of five thousand pounds.

This silent market in black worth is pervasive. When a certain brand of hiking boots became popular among young people in Harlem, the manufacturer pulled the product from inner-city stores, fearing that such a trend would 'ruin' the image of their boot among the larger market of whites.

It's funny. . . even shoes.

Last year I had a funny experience in a shoe store. The salesman would only bring me one shoe, not two.

'I can't try on a pair?' I asked in disbelief.

'When you pay for a pair,' he retorted. 'What if there were a hundred of you,' he continued. 'How would we keep track?'

I was the only customer in the store, but there were a hundred of me in his head.

In our Anglo-American jurisprudence there is a general constraint limiting the right to sue to cases and controversies affecting the individual. As an individual, I could go to the great and ridiculous effort of suing for the miniscule amount at stake in waiting for the other shoe to drop from his hand; but as for the real claim, the group claim, the larger defamation to all those other hundreds of me. . . well, that will be a considerably tougher row to hoe.

I am one, I am many.

I am amiable, orderly, extremely honest, and a very good neighbour indeed. I am suspect profile, market cluster, actuarial monster, statistical being.

My particulars battle the generals.

'Typecasting!' I protest.
'Predictive indicator,' assert the keepers of the gate.
'Prejudice!' I say.
'Precaution,' they reply.
Hundreds, even thousands, of me hover in the breach.

4

The War Between the Worlds

A friend is wearily discussing her marital woes. Of her husband she says: 'He's the sort of person who'll have a conversation with me, but in his head. It'll turn into a huge imaginary fight in which I wound, offend or disappoint him repeatedly. At some random point he'll re-enter real life in order to track me down in the laundry room so that he can set me straight.'

On some level, talking about race is a lot like having a conversation with an abusive spouse. The igniting spark may be small but the stakes great, the blaze of emotion rendering each impossible to please, the fight not really about whatever the fight is about. A war between the real and the imagined, the remembered and the fantasised, the likely and the outrageous.

'You're stupid!' Through the radiator pipes of my hotel room comes the voice of an anonymous, quarrelling neighbour. I sit in my suite, reading a cross-section of popular newspapers and magazines. A best-selling book claims to have proved anew that blacks and poor people are more stupid than everyone else. . . Or, as they put it 'genetically inferior' to the rest of humanity. . .

'Who gave you the right to say anything!' comes the voice again. I bury myself in my reading: *Middle class Negroes talk too much. Those in poverty are illiterate loudmouths. Real black people struggle silently, mute in the noble choice of their lumpen libertarianism.*

'I pay the bills around here.' *Whites pay all the taxes, blacks do all the spending. White people are sacrificial; black people are greedy and grasping.*

'You can just get out and be homeless if you're so unhappy.' *Blacks who find it so hard being around whites should just move back to the ghetto so they can focus their attentions more handily upon some real problems.*

'You're a tramp!' *Today's black civil rights activists are pimps, cheap pretenders to a moral vision, interested only in the mountains of gain and glory to be made by selling out the legacy of that great conservative statesmen Martin Luther King, whose most famous lost quotation was, 'Why Don't We Go Get a Real Job.'*

'You're sick!' *Black culture is endlessly pathological; whites are therefore rational in their racism.*

'You're a cry-baby! Stop whining!' says the voice in the wall. Says an editorial: *Blacks are professional victims, always complaining, always ungrateful.*

There's the sound of a slap and a yelp.

'You deserved that!' *Blacks get more than they deserve.*

'So sue me!' growls the voice. *Discrimination suits that result in judicial awards of damages are 'corporate muggings', and 'racial shakedowns'.*

I wonder whether to call the police.

Woody Allen, film-maker and narcissist extraordinaire, once came up with the syllogism to end all syllogisms: God is good. I am good. Therefore I am God. That form of logical thought, employed to preposterous ends, characterises much of contemporary debate about racial science, to say nothing of a host of easy social and political equations in which some are, shall we say, more than a little invested. . .

Too often of late the media has been flooded with studies purporting to 'inform' us of the inherent inequality, inferiority and preordained undeservingness of this or that group. The studies are always based on the beliefs of lots of experts, a few of whom may just happen to be Nazis, but not to worry, *real* science is unsullied by such things. Those Nazi screeds, those slavery manifestos are dusted right off and tidied up into neat statistical columns, with rows of impressive numbers, dotted with decimal points, percentage signs hovering at the edges like so much filigree. Often, there is a little show of cost benefit analysis, the utility of genetic superiority always outweighing 'whatever bias there may be'. Genetic and cultural superiority are declared the cornerstones of true meritocracy.

Egalitarianism, alas, finds itself huddling on a street corner, reviled as relativism, and begging for bread. The high-minded pseudo-scientists are sure to make known the unfathomable depths of their most sympathetic sensibilities. Regrettably, their pseudo-findings are propelled, against their will of course, by the inevitability and weight of sheer pseudo-*facts*; propelled to the inhospitable unpleasantness of the ultimate pseudo-conclusion.

One of the great difficulties with pseudo-science is that it is so hard to refute just by saying it isn't so. The logical structure – if not substance – of pseudo-science posits what purports to be fact; it requires counter-fact to make counter-argument. Black people find themselves responding endlessly to such studies before we can be heard on any other subject; we must credentialise ourselves as number-crunching social scientists quickly in order to be seen as even minimally intelligent. That's the catch: racial science makes anyone who agrees with it intelligent, enhanced, informed and empowered. Real numbers, real science – it's what school teaches us to revere. And it makes anyone who knows the great messy, unprovable contrary, who knows the indecipherable complexity of black or white people, who knows the reality and potential of all humanity – us silly egalitarians – it makes us unintelligent, uninformed, powerless and naïve.

Some few do attempt the counter-studies. Some few attempt the studies attacking assertions that identical twins share genes for becoming chimney-sweeps. Some few wearily pursue the studies countering cited similarities between the bone structure of dinosaurs and inner-city youth. But none of this really deals with the attributional assumptions underlying the debate about black people and white people. In fact it almost underscores or enhances the idea that all this psychological battering is just a matter that scientists can resolve. It narrows the debate to the property of (extra-intelligent) 'experts' who wrap their opinions in the sheepskin of false 'proof'.

But race involves slippages of logic at many levels other than at these exalted heights. Consider this rather banal scenario: a white child of my acquaintance said to his black schoolmate, 'I wish I could be black so I could play basketball as well as you.' The black child was offended and told his parents about the remark. The parents of the black child approached the parents of the white child and, rather testily, asked them to tell their offspring that playing basketball is not an inherently black thing. The mother of the white child came to me for intercession, complaining that the parents of the black child wouldn't speak to her anymore.

'What happened? ' I asked.

'Nothing,' she responded. 'I just told them that it was true that blacks play better basketball than anyone else. After all,' she continued, 'anyone can turn on TV and see that any basketball player worth talking about just happens to be black.'

It's hard work, the fallacies underlying such encounters. Well-meaning people trying to be liberal, yet the Woody Allen syllogism bedevilling at every turn: *Everyone I see playing bas-ketball is black. Everyone playing basketball must be black. If I am not black, I can't play basketball; if you are black, you must be a basketball player.*

Or as a three-year-old neighbour put it upon returning from seeing the movie *Space Jam*, a simple-minded drama in which Warner Brothers cartoon characters battle space aliens on the basketball court: 'Everyone who plays basketball is named Michael Jordan,' she said, so sweetly, so innocently, yet so precariously. None of us is immune. . .

I confess, it's very hard to talk about race or ethnicity or class these days, when myths, clichés and bromides have so overrun the discourse: when blacks or the poor are only par-tially real, inhabiting as they do an imaginary landscape of tendentious disputation; when women or Bangledeshis are great blurry windmills whose gigantic arms are thought to be churning in a most threatening manner; when Catholics or Muslims are those whose gargantuan mouths spew gritty clouds of chaff.

Rational*ised* racism has become the soup of the day; race is said to determine IQ; IQ is supposed to determine economic status. (This is the logic that made Pamela Anderson and Tommy Lee a wealthy couple, I suppose. Brains, brains and more brains.)

Personally, I want nothing more than to move on to the promised land of colour-blind milk and honey produced by only the most qualified of worker bees. Yet. . . at moments like this it's so hard to imagine. It's hard to keep one's concentra-tion when, phoenix-like, the rooster of racial science rises every twenty years or so, in ever more seductive plumage, intent upon proving the lost link between the rising of the sun and its crowing loudly. Like clockwork black people must put aside the activities of everyday life and subject ourselves to the cyclical inspection point of proving our worth, justifying our existence, and teaching our history, over and over and over again.

This enervating nonsense depends, of course, upon leaving unexamined the fluctuating categorisation at play in determining who is *permitted* to be white, who marked as black. In the United States, those deemed touched by the superstition of colour have included, at various moments in history, Native Americans, Jews, Eastern and Southern Europeans, and Portuguese. In the United Kingdom, the category has expanded and contracted around immigrant groups such as Africans, Caribbeans, Bangledeshis, Pakistanis and Indians. And if Afro-Caribbeans are tagged by some as 'the New Irish', then surely we must include the old Irish.

An anthropologist friend of mine tells me the story of a Haitian statesman who was visited by an official from the United States during the 1930s. 'What percentage of Haiti's population is white?' asked the American. Ninety-five per cent, came the answer. The American official was flustered and assuming that the Haitian was mistaken exclaimed, 'I don't understand – how on earth do you come up with such a figure?'

'Well, how do you measure blackness in the United States?'

'Anyone with a black ancestor.'

'Well, that's exactly how we measure whiteness,' retorted the Haitian.

If we really think about it, the very category of something called 'whiteness' is revealed as a kind of collective neural toboggan run, encouraging good people to slide, to *shush* at high speed right on through the realm of reason. Whiteness is a kind of sociological clubhouse, a weird compression of tribal and ethnic animosities, some dating back to the time of the Roman invasions, all realigned to make new enemies, all compromised to make new friends. East against west, north against south, high against low, light against dark, black against white. The notion of whiteness as any kind of racial purity is a cognitive blind spot blocking out the pain, as far as I can make any sense at all of it, of such histories as the

Thirty Years' War, massacres in Scotland and tyranny in Transylvania. Buttressed by aesthetic trends that feel ever-so-inherent, we can't slow down to think to save our lives.

In some quarters these days, the discussion of biracialism has taken hold as a concept containing the seeds of hope for future harmony. What the term usually refers to is a person of a mixed marriage, 'mixed' almost always meaning the product of one white parent and one black or Asian parent. Love will show us the way, is the bottom line of this argument. Perhaps. But what troubles me is the degree to which few people in the world, and most particularly in the United States, are anything *but* multiracial, to say nothing of merely *bi*racial. The use of this term seems to privilege the offspring of mixed marriage as those 'between' races without doing much to enhance the social status of all us mixed-up products of the illegitimacies of the not-so-distant past.

As much as I celebrate the future of a culturally mixed, biologically miscegenous world, therefore, I worry that we seem genuinely unable to appreciate how much we are already in that happy state of nature. If we do not at present see the overlapping profusion of unions that are encompassed within the category 'black' as well as 'white', then the vaunting of a new *bi*racialism becomes nothing more than the embrace of the same old caste systems as new and legitimate. With the pinning of racial hope upon blood mixtures in such a literal way, moreover, there comes a sneaky sort of implied duty to assimilate – the duty to grab on to the DNA ladder and hoist oneself onward and upward.

I have a cousin who is relatively light-skinned – however one measures these things – and whose appearance has always confused some who derive a sense of security from knowing who is on what side of the great racial divide. I remember her telling me about an encounter she had had with one of her university professors. When the professor discovered she was a member of the black law students' association, he grew agitated, annoyed, even confrontive. Why would she do such a thing, he wanted to know; why would she 'label' herself when she was so light-skinned and could so easily pass for white? My cousin was struck by how offended he was; he seemed to be implying that she had an obligation or a duty to pass and that her failure to do so was both impolitic and impolite.

But what was being urged was a model of assimilation in which one's heritage became either a secret or a burden. And like all family secrets, that is a model with devastating repercussive consequence. Let me offer an example of such secrecy in a somewhat different context.

Two years ago I visited the campus of an elite liberal arts college in New England. I have one frozen visual image from that visit, a very clear recollection of seeing a smiling young black woman moving into a sorority house. Sororities and fraternities are a kind of exclusive, invitation-only eating club pervasive on American campuses. There she was, this new black member in an overwhelmingly white sorority on an overwhelmingly white campus. She was wearing Bermuda shorts and the ubiquitous sweatshirt emblazoned with the university logo; her nails were painted a serious shade of red; her chemically smoothed hair was drawn back into a little tuft of ponytail. She was unloading her belongings from a Volkswagen. She carried a large stuffed Snoopy dog and a bulging cosmetics case. She looked eager, young and very happy.

The reason this image is so indelibly etched is that shortly afterwards, I had a conversation with a white student at that college, who assured me that there were no racial problems in universities anymore. You are living in the past, she assured me. I was just about to give myself over to this good future when she began to describe how her sorority had admitted black people for *years* now, although it was true that the national chapter just charged local chapters a little more for black members. It was the way she said it that so floored me: no racism, just some extra pocket money tucked like a good motherly caution into a subordinate clause.

She did not seem to have any idea how deeply distressing I found this information. She talked about it as though they were buying accessories – a special fund for decorating each house with a few black faces, to be strewn about for accent, like scatter pillows. The notion that such a charge also operated as a *dis*incentive in financial hard times did not seem to have impressed her with the dimension of that moral corruption. But it was a terribly sad commentary, this tax that assumed not only that black members cost more, but that the new black members would never know about it, would never learn what goes on with the treasury; this complaisant fee schedule that assumed, indeed required, that no black people will ever rise to the national chapter's inner circle.

I think about the betrayal of that young black woman, with such a well-kept secret. She, so great a liability, so to speak, that her handling fees went through the roof. (And knowing of her plight myself, should I not rationally wonder about the hidden transaction costs of my own associations? Would that make me paranoid?) How do we proceed in a world where race operates as a hidden scripting of rationalised irrationality, where myriad images of racial clichés perpetuate their unspoken subtexts of devaluation?

A few years ago, conservative author Shelby Steele wrote that American black people had better find the means to pay the price of a ticket before boarding the proverbial freedom train. With this complicated imagery of liberty with a price tag, the metaphors of the Civil Rights Movement met their cruel and convulsive end upon the spot. This notion of freedom's surcharge became a pun, in which the liberatory movement of a people only a few generations from slavery was transformed into the equivalent of an economic gratuity in which free agency, free market and political autonomy have been terminally confused. In this ironic gesture, racial hierarchies have been recirculated and resold, again with the assistance of those familiar henchmen, sociobiology, econometric theories of rational behaviour and other totalising claims.

The legacy of slavery's dehumanisation of black people has been carried forward in such a variety of cultural contexts. Racism is coded differently in the north of the United States than in the south; in the east of Canada than in the west, in the north of London than in the east. I mentioned in an earlier lecture that race often *defines* class in the American context. There is no lower class than being black. And among so many consequences of slavery and segregation surely one of the most remarkable has been the effective conflation of myriad ethnic identities engendered by the construction of whiteness as its own form of nationalism.

Throughout the twentieth century, these habits of thought have skewed public discussions of such topics as 'the underclass' and immigration in remarkably powerful ways. The welfare debate in the United States has been driven almost entirely by the manipulation of racial rather than class images – primarily images of the endlessly reproductive, devouring wombs of black women – the ubiquitous myths of their 'take-over' bodies, so rolling with an engulfment of forbidden flesh, yet even that hyperbolic femaleness never breaking into the realm of the feminine.

To the contrary, the 'strong' libidinously-endowed black woman is more often depicted as a kind of androgynous or even masculine force. Consistently denied any archetypal function as parenting her own children, she is relentlessly figured not just as a bad mother, but one who seeks motherhood only as the 'lazy' person's escape from her true place, best measured by long years of impecunious servitude to others. This fearsome image of the poor black teenage pregnant 'welfare queen' has facilitated the removal of social benefits for all women: i.e., the replacement of traditional welfare programmes with so-called 'workfare' programmes, as well as the denial of additional benefits to poor women who have children while on public assistance.

Black people seem to be emerging as a kind of great global surplus, now that we are no longer chattels and in demand as such. Black people are seen as thieves in the warehouse of human bounty. Perhaps this framing explains the peculiar forms of economic growth attending the incarceration of disproportionate numbers of young black men: from the prison construction industry to the reinstitution of chain gangs to the burgeoning unionisation of police, to effectively organised and high-powered lobbying efforts of prison guards. Indeed, prisons have emerged as the most rapidly expanding area of public sector growth in the United States.

As in the context of welfare, it is startling to look critically at the political uses of prison 'work' as a purported 'lesson' in an economy that offers the least skilled of this society – black or white – few to no jobs in the 'free' market sector. It is startling to look at the data of racially disproportionate rates of incarceration, and the implications of such data in the context of such punishments as chain gangs – that is, forms of punishment that serve principally as public shaming ceremonies. Black people are wealth that can be thrown away, human capital that may be discarded conspicuously, the conspicuous consumption of black bodies in synchrony with their conspicuous discard.

I very much hope that I am wrong, but sometimes I fear that the United State's unfortunate taste for bread and circus in the politics of racial division has emerged as one of its hottest export items in the new global marketplace – the O.J. Simpson case alone. . . Whether dressed up as 'news', 'entertainment', 'sport' or 'science' the new rationalised irrationality of race is almost always also 'big business,' one endless shell game of race, class, ethnicity, culture and identity played one against the other.

Yet even as the very rhetorical form of the Civil Rights Movement's best successes are being both copied and co-opted so variously that both the new South African government and a variety of new white-rights movements can claim to be the beneficiaries of its persuasive voice and moral vision, so the political and legal claims of the 1960s and 1970s have been made to seem the 'inefficient', 'greedy' graspings of those in need of a good cost-benefit analysis.

It's hard this work. I remember seeing an article a few years ago about how some intelligence organisation or other had developed drugs that change melanin concentration or some such, so that agents and spies could change races. It sounded awfully like science fiction to me, and I cite it here not for the truth of the matter, but for its evocative allure in the realm of social, if not science, fiction – this body-snatching for high espionage.

What would it mean to change races, particularly from the perspective of so-called intelligence agents? Do they have teams of transracials who are poised to infiltrate the race-house of cards? What would a white man tinted black in order to sabotage blackness find himself thinking? And wouldn't blackness just end up sabotaging him everytime he walked down the street? Would he have to turn himself back into a white person in order to file his report with the powers that be? Would his insights be valued the same way if he reported for duty looking that look?

An acquaintance of mine who works in the fashion indus-try told me of an occasion that looks at the issue from a slightly different angle. A group of high fashion models, including lone black supermodel Naomi Campbell, were, as he put it, 'whited up' for some fashion shoot; the issue of race and Campbell's difference seemed to disappear beneath the heavily chalky make-up, concluded this observer.

But I wonder if race would have 'disappeared' as he put it, if we reversed the image: if all the models had been, how would one say it, 'blacked down'? (For if the models were whited upwards in the first instance, are they not blacked down in the second? The hierachies of colour are so insistently built into the habits of our language.)

And what of whiting *out*? As when Ford Motor Company 'whited out' the brown British faces in an advertisement it ran in Poland? Are we really accommodating different audiences or are we erasing that which must be repressed? It is hard, this work.

The limp little tag hanging from my teabag reads: 'It's easy to be tolerant when you do not care.'

A jumble of dreams in the last few days: I sit at my desk, I am writing this lecture. I reach for a little bottle of a correctional fluid called White-Out, I start brushing it over the last few sentences. My fingers start to dissolve. In seconds, my index finger and little finger of my right hand are almost completely melted away, to the knuckle, and the others are down to the first joint. There is no pain; I just watch them disappear quietly, quickly, as though they are no longer part of me.

It is the subtlest of sensations.

An Ordinary Brilliance: Parting the Waters, Closing the Wounds

This is the year when Europe re-dedicates itself to the eradication of racism, xenophobia and anti-Semitism. I have presented these lectures in the spirit of that dedication and with the hope that the productive controversy my words undoubtedly will have stirred will continue. Will continue around dinner tables, will continue as little shifts of empathy, will occasion some degree of thought-provoking anxiety and yet remain. . . civil.

My assumption in these lectures has been that my audience is one of good people of all races and ages, good people of good will. And my subject has been the small aggressions of unconscious racism, rather than the big-booted oppressions of bigotry in its most extreme manifestations. I have chosen to speak of these quieter forms of racism because I think that the eradication of prejudice, the reconciling of tensions across racial, ethnic, cultural and religious lines depends upon eradicating the little blindnesses, not just the big. It depends upon eradicating the troublesome attitudinal divide between the paralysing anxiety of well-meaning 'white guilt' and the smouldering unhappiness of blacks who dare not speak their minds. It is not an easy project this. Perhaps as an outsider it will have been easier for me to raise these issues; if so, I hope my thoughts will be a bridge to the more intimate contexts of the struggles you face in a specifically British context.

To summarise some of the points that I think are most important.

Race is not a cipher for poverty. Racism is no doubt immensely complicated by the privations of poverty, but, like anti-Semitism, xenophobia and gender bias, it has a separate power that transgresses socio-economic strata. *Race is not the same as poverty*.

Race is not a cipher for disease. I am thinking of the globally renowned geneticist who, at a luncheon I attended recently, said: 'Unfortunately, AIDS may be the answer to Africa's social problems.' Too many people are enamoured of Malthusian explanations for racism, plague and pestilence as just convenient forms of natural selection. *Race is not a cipher for disease*.

Race is not a cipher for bestiality. Reject, I beseech you, all those dehumanising stereotypes of big baboons, so insulting even to baboons: small-brained, aggressive, excessively sized body parts, brightly coloured hindquarters advertising endless sexual availability, possessed of a boisterous personality and a taste for sensual delights with no moderating instinct for propriety. Resist, I say to you, those images whose metaphoric power has dehumanised blacks, has dehumanised Jews before that, has dehumanised all who utter such ugliness into continued being. *Race is not a cipher for the subhuman*.

Race is not a cipher for exotic entertainment. All you who have endured the trample of tourists violating your little corner of paradise in search of ancient abbeys, imagine how it feels to *be* the monument in question, to *be* the 'flavour of the day', the plumed endangered species with the band around one's ankle. It is a kind of deep disrespect, this failure to see the difference between my humanity, for instance, and the seductiveness of a moss-covered ruin. . . 'I am part Native

American,' I told someone recently. His eyebrows went up as though I were a particularly romantic bit of architectural rubble. '*Really*,' he said, with a breathy thrill in his voice, and a quiver of excitement that told me he had never met one of *those* before. He lifted his hand up in the international signal for 'Cigar Store Indian'. 'How!' he said in a deep voice, and with the reverent solemnity of a duck hunter emitting one of those calls that attracts the kind of ducks whose goose will no doubt soon be cooked. *Race is not a cipher for exotic entertainment.*

Race is not a cipher for the whole of life. When I speak of race you must bear in mind that this is not the same thing as saying that race explains everything. Race does not explain all forms of misfortune any more than it explains the colour of one's socks. Yet conversations about race so quickly devolve into anxious bouts of wondering why we are not talking about something – anything – else, like hard work or personal responsibility or birth order or class or God or the good, old glories of the human spirit. All these are worthy topics of conversation, surely, but. . . can we consider, for just one moment, *race*.

I am often pressed to stop considering so much and just to think up a nice set of snappy solutions. But racism is an enormously subtle perceptual matter. Shifting its perceptions involves figuring out how to insinuate one's way through all sorts of well-guarded social hierarchies that affect blacks no less than whites. There is an oft-cited story of a well-dressed black man who boards a train. A white person announces with distaste, 'There's a Negro on this train.' The black man leaps up in alarm as says 'Where? Where?'

Finding a door *in* is a trick of social vision as much as it is of legal remedy or political recourse.

How do I startle someone into seeing racism, even when it indicts oneself. How do I, in effect, tickle someone into seeing the links between: the sensation of lowered status when a black person sits down at the next table in the restaurant; the sensation of economic risk when a black face is advertising the product you produce; the sensation of certainty that no black person has anything at all to teach you.

If and when that seeing happens, that seeing of an unconsidered link to racism – it comes one way in the first instance, sneaks up, soft as osmosis in the second, crashes through with a bright flash in the third. The understanding never seems to happen in the same way twice. That's why I offer not a single set of pronouncements, but a layered set of parables for what I hope will be sensible and sustained *consideration*.

This contemporary see-sawing between the capitulation to a sense of inevitable doom and the frenetically applied 'quick fix' is a phenomenon of which I am extremely suspicious. Impatience rather than urgency guides the thinking. Pressing problems are met not with deeper thought, just quicker thought. In fact I would go so far as to say that part of what is actually aggravates social and racial divisions at the moment is precisely that deep current of doom over which babbles a stream of simplistic bromides, such as 'just love one another!' 'family values!' and 'victimology!' Hard to argue with; hard to analyse; and hardly a substitute for serious engagement.

I believe that race shares a pattern with other -isms, a relation to other hierarchies. It is, I think, why the lessons of the Holocaust are important to the entire world, why the Civil Rights Movement became a model in the uprising in Tiennamen Square, why the struggle for black equality has sustained so much piggy backing with other movements.

It is helpful to remember that, for all its diffuseness, the power of race as dangerous and sensational has been perpetuated by very identifiable historical phenomena. Racism is not inevitable, however entrenched. There have been better and worse moments in the history of race relations. Race as an invested feature of modern relations is scarcely much older than the triangle trade. Understanding this as a relatively recent phenomenon reveals how many of our racial clashes are the consequence of human shipwreck rather than divine order. It is my optimistic conviction that the more of this history we study, the more we can map the shoals upon which we are likely to become stranded, the more nuanced our responses and the more salutory the outcomes.

This sounds simpler and more obvious than perhaps it is. Surely there has not been much respect or regard for this as academic enterprise; 'political correctness!' comes the dismissive hiss. This is very much society's loss. I think that the psychic and physical devastation that so marked slave and colonial systems echoes into our lives today, a traumatic reiteration among both blacks and whites. If we could but see a causal chain, a procession of events linked over time, it might teach us many lessons about the long-term consequences of violently exploiting humans as only capital, of exhausting them to death, and then treating their bodies like interchangeable, worn-out machines.

I think that a significant part of the failure to see each other is fed by a persistently divided rhetoric of race. In this regard, the intertwined roles of pseudo-science and the organs of mass culture in perpetuating those ideologies of violence deserve close scrutiny. For an example of such divided thought, consider those instances of criminals who are black and raise little armies. They are called gangs. They are called pathological, brutish and incapable of comprehending social limit. Criminals who are white and raise little armies are too often seen as rugged individuals, beleaguered patriots, militiamen pursuing new frontiers, a little misguided perhaps but honourable. Both are surely outlaws, yet tellingly, both tend to be romanticised within their various communities as outposts against the encroaching excess of big government and state force.

This employ of differentiated racial rhetoric, not just for general predictive guidance, but to indict real individuals as though by real description – this has been fueled by the very powerful forces of racial science. We must be on our guard for this new race science, the science of stereotypification, so outlandishly well-funded at the moment, so skilled at flooding the ever more narrowly-controlled media, so seductive to those who need easy explanations for the seemingly uncontrollable forces so rapidly shaping our world. I have tried to introduce, over the course of these lectures, specific examples of how racial stereotype masquerades as scientific category; I hope those examples provide a general cautionary lesson about how popular culture in every era has mythologised racial myth into a kind of felt normativity powerful enough to trump even the most compelling empirical data.

As a beneficiary of so many of the gains of the Civil Rights Movement in the United States, I believe that the commitment to the notion of equality has been the very cornerstone of that progress. Certainly there have been many battles about how one defines equality – equality of outcome? Equality of access to the basic necessities of life like food, health care, education and housing? Equality as neutral, colour-blind principle? Or equality as substantive equity and fairness before the law? But however fractious that argument has been, one of the most ominous turns in the American debate of late has been an open and growing abandon of even the ideal of egalitarianism. 'We are *not* all equal,' comes the plaint. 'Why even pretend?' Then a list of entitlements based on being 'better than' and other perogatives of power. Inherent superiority, masquerading as merit, is then used to attack entitlement programmes allocating resources to the disempowered.

The resistance to egalitarianism is also a product of the insecurities of this global economic moment. The values of a resolutely efficient market-place are not always compatible with the principles of fairness. And while there is something to be said for distributive justice theories of dog-eat-dog and *caveat emptor* in the inanimate context of a sale of ball bearings, I do not wish to see that dynamic overtake our entire ethical, civil and political discourse. There is nothing wrong with the idea of market economics given its own historical context and some negotiated normative limits. But when our very self-worth becomes linked to our material possessions, when poor or socially undesired people become discardable because they are deemed useless, we *must* retain our sense of alarm about such a state. Our definition of human utility *must* be broader and more generous. In these times of broad polemic we must revivify the struggle, the love and the logic that gave birth to the ideas and the implementation of egalitarianism.

Finally, I would like to return to what I think is one of the greatest obstacles to progress at this moment – the paralysing claim that racism *has* no solution. Resembling often the schoolyard game of bullies tormenting those deemed wimps, this argument takes a number of forms:

Racism is not a problem because racism is 'universal', *all* cultures are racist and xenophobic. Circling the wagons around one's own is just a 'human thing'.

Or: Racism is not a problem because even if it is a problem, it's a *social* problem, and law, politics and economic regulation have no place in the social realm. 'People' will just have to deal with it 'by themselves'. Let them inter-marry. Not quite let them eat cake, but rather a romantic resolution to palpable political disparity.

Or: Racism isn't a problem because while white people *used* to hate black people, now it's black people who hate white people, so it's only fair for white people to hate black people in return. And so the argument sloshes back and forth, forth and back, like a pendulum, like a lullaby, like the tolling of a bell.

Or: Racism is a problem, but it's not *our* problem. Black people ought to help themselves before they lay claim to the sympathies of good white people. I must say, I always wonder at this sifting out of the presumed responsibility of black people for their own fate, that so casually overlooks the long history self-help and intra-community networks that do exist. Such self-help structures, churches for example, are neither wealthy nor philanthropic in a way that matches those of some other groups, but much political rhetoric treats them as non-existent. And while no one can argue that black self-help is not a fine thing, I wonder about its meaning when it is used as an injunction that black concerns be severed from the ethical question of how we as a society operate. These debates make me suspicious when they are raised so as to be at the core of arguments about black people overreaching, even as black people earn only two-thirds of similarly educated and qualified white people. These arguments fuel characterisations of anti-discrimination remedies as only having helped those who were already overprivileged to begin with; they feed images of those who speak publicly of racial discrimination as those who are merely 'shaking down' the establishment, exploiting white guilt for personal profit.

With regard to all these configurations, let me just say that I am certain that the solution to racism lies in our ability to see its ubiquity but not concede its inevitability. It lies in the collective and institutional power to make change, at least as much as with the individual will to change. It also lies in the absolute moral imperative to break the childish, deadly circularity of centuries of blindness to the shimmering brilliance of our common, ordinary humanity.

I do believe wholeheartedly that there are lessons to be gleaned from the practised commitment to the community of all people. What is it that enables a discourse of hospitality when we step across the boundaries to be part of a world other than our own. How unrestrained – or imperial – is the claim of what we call ours in the world? When I come to London, albeit in the fizzy-cultural wake of the singer Michael Jackson, when you come to the churches of Harlem – how gracefully do we negotiate the accommodation of each other's presence even as the lurking threat of such accommodation is loss – our sacrifice in knowing that inclusion of new faces might change the landscape forever.

On one hand, how can we make each other welcome in a world in which fear so rules the day; on the other hand, how can we present ourselves responsibly so as not to wear thin the welcome mat in a world that is increasingly, urgently, and perhaps irreversibly diasporic. On one hand, how do we maintain the rituals, the mother tongues, the intimacies that reinforce the boundaries of what keeps us sane. On the other hand, how do we remain open to the possibility that my son may want to marry your daughter. (Although. . . I must say in my own case the greater test would come if my son were to become affianced to the aforesaid Jackson offspring.)

Perhaps part of this is, in the words of an old Cherokee proverb, as simple as trying to walk a mile in another's mocassins. Just the momentary imaginary exercise of taking to mind and heart the investment of oneself in another, indeed the investment of oneself as that other.

This simplicity is in tension with the hard part, of course, the task of summoning up the generosity it takes to scrunch down a few inches in the family pew in order to make room for the funny-looking newcomer. And even that task is mere metaphor for the *really* hard part, that of facing the possibility of the elimination of one's community as distinct, and of one's heralded bloodline as a pure inheritance.

In the United States, there is a battle, glibly called 'the culture wars' in which fearsome conjurings of motley and mongrel immigrant values are counterposed to the visionary seamlessness of a mythical American cultural unity which is in turn vaunted as a tradition of unalloyed Englishness. Of course, the degree to which the United States has long been one big, chunky, simmering stew of alloy is perhaps most apparent to those of us who are most proud of our distinctly flavourful contributions to the American broth. But, as in the context of miscegenation, the extent to which an always pre-existing alloy is celebrated as pure in any given historical moment is the extent to which we suppress the history of a kind of primal human struggle: a struggle between the embracing familiarity of the narrow well-worn path, as opposed to the heady vastness, the liberating lure of human universalism.

The extent to which we are always becoming one another even as we defend our difference to the death was nowhere more apparent to me than last summer, when I was invited to attend one of the May Balls at Cambridge University. 'The Director's Ball,' read the invitation, and the theme was a spirited spoof of Hollywood, with takeoffs of films like *007*, and *9½ Weeks*, *The Juror*, *Seargent Bilko* and *Fantasy Island*. There were lots of odd creatures, emerging from the Cam amidst the punting boats – damsels in distress, lost actors, submarines and monsters. The college grounds had been given over to casinos, massage parlours, grunge bands, strobe lights. . . Oh, and the velcro catapult. This is an odd contraption I have never seen in America, the object of which is to don a costume covered in velcro strips, get a running start upon a gigantic trampoline and propel oneself through the air in such a way as to apply one's person to a giant inflatable velcro bullseye. It was quite a sight, this spectacle of future prime ministers vaulting through the air in evening wear and rubber cat suits. With their white ties tucked primly within the velcro jumpsuits, a run, run, run, a leap, a boing and a bound, they flipped through the air – splitch! There they hung, lopsided, upsidedown, bobbling like giant fuzzy tennis balls upon the obesely undulating air mattress of a velcro scoreboard.

There'll always be an England, I suppose. On the other hand, what did it mean that *I* was there, even thinking that thought, so amused and vaguely repelled?

Were those *real* Pepsi machines at the ends of every corridor? Or imported for the night?

Nonetheless, this was 'a *very* British affair', I have been informed subsequently. 'We British are amused and yet repelled by American-ness', I was told; 'that May Ball was making *fun* of Americans.'

It was helpful, that. Imitation is one thing, making fun another. I began to understand the disconnection I was feeling, a feeling of being caught in a tumbling kaleidescope of weird American slices, little shards of multiple stereotypes tossing about in a glittering tunnel of slap-dash parody.

'Are you one of the dancers?' I was asked at one point. The question cut through my dawning understanding that imitation alone is a pretty complicated thing; for imitation risks becoming.

'Are you one of the dancers?' I was standing on the edge of a room full of lethargic Cantabridgians in elegant gowns; they were gazing at half a dozen, hired ballroom dancers dressed in sequinned outfits twirling like Fred Astaire and Ginger Rogers. The observers seemed bored yet transfixed, in the way of voyeurs, as though they were watching a distant thing. The dancers spun wordlessly and repetitively, as blithe and mechanical as figurines atop a wedding cake.

Why are the dancers dancing? I wondered. Why are the others not dancing? And, *am I one of the dancers?*

I wandered on, lost in a kind of fractured familiarity. What does it *mean*, I asked with the persistent repetitivenes of the idiot savant; what is the meaning of that falafel stand, those Gummy Bears, that wall-sized poster of Demi Moore?

Since then, I have tried to figure out if my presence at the Cambridge May Ball was a little like those tourists at a Harlem church. I don't suppose there were enough of me to forcefully impose the kind of lopsided power dynamic that makes for good voyeurism, particularly since I was so busy passing as one of the hired dancers. But as I wandered innocently through those re-enactments of scenes from the film *9¹/₂ Weeks*, I was moved to much meditation upon the enormous power imbalances embedded in the vocabulary with which we ritualistically delineate community, between being asked to dance and being one of 'the' dancers. The differences between black and white, between gang and militia, between what is deemed in our own interest and what foreign, between what we figure as legitimate and what we cast out as illegitimate, between what we see and what we know, between what we say and what we do.

There are sudden moments in my life that I realise that I exist within the shadow of a public preconception. The little jolt of realising what you symbolise is pathological dispossession and the ultimate in alienability. The 'we', of which I am part, are those who can be uprooted and put down anywhere. We can be experimented with and replanted and cut down and still we will spring back like weeds in the Garden of Eden.

With a shock, I see that 'I' am seen a bit like Gulliver, stomping my way among the Lilliputions. The earth trembles beneath my feet and there is a grinding, snapping, crunching of tiny dwellings as I walk. Little people, *good* little Lilliputions, are fleeing for their lives.

But living as a preconception is a variable condition, and seconds later, I come to find myself in the land of the Gargantuans, dodging the soles of big-footed giants, my voice an insignificant squeak, unheard no matter how I shout. Oh. Am I shouting? With a shock I find I am huge again. I have shifted once more, travelled through the Looking Glass, Alice in Wonderland, like Mighty Mouse, the contours of my body inflate and shrink, wither and bloat, according to the vagaries of public mood. Oh. You can't hear me. There. How's that. I am trying *so* hard to be normal.

Am I fiction? Am I real? Is there a she, is there a me, apart from this bad dream?

This distance between the self, and the drama of one's stereotype; the distance between the nice internal spirit that is no one but oneself, and this wild image of projected fear. Negotiating that distance is an ethical project of creating a livable space between the poles of other people's imagination and the nice calm centre of oneself where dignity resides. Creating and negotiating that space is the work of what I think of as the question at the centre of our resolution of racism, of xenophobia and anti-Semitism and a host of other -isms.

This is the question that ultimately informs the spirit that makes us all human, the spirit that worries for our dignity. This spirit that animates us as community.

I dream of a house, a dream house, my great-grandmother's house, the house on the corner of a hot street in a small town suspended in time. My grandmother's plates. Her cherry music stand, her silver spoons, my mother's books. Each room is filled with dreams and memories and the continuity I feel through them. The sense of precariousness in knowing that this simple thread is all there ever is.

Home. Each place I have lived like a skin, like a protection, like a shelter not against the weather, but against the gaze of the world, an eyrie from which to contemplate what has happened in a day.

There can be no freedom for any of us, I suppose, untempered by the incumbency to hold oneself both open and yet back a bit, to hold oneself in the posture of one regarding something larger than Oneself, an attitude of restraint, a habit of awe.

And within that freedom we may yet find miracles – miracles, I think, a metaphor for the insight that comes with the lack of prejudice, the abandon of pre-judgement, the willingness to see another viewpoint and be converted if only for a moment, to allow oneself be held in a state of suspended knowing.

Culturally, blackness signifies the realm of the always known, as well as the not worth knowing. A space of the entirely judged. This prejudice is a practice of the non-religious; it is profane, the ultimate profanity of presuming to know it all. Racism is a gaze that insists upon the power to make others conform, to perform endlessly in the prison of prior expectation, circling repetitively back upon the expired utility of the entirely known. Our rescue, our deliverance perhaps, lies in the possibility of listening across that great divide, of being surprised by the Unknown, by the unknowable. Old habits of being given way, let us hope, to a gentler genealogy of Grace.